50 King Fisherman Ocean Cuisine Recipes

By: Kelly Johnson

Table of Contents

- Grilled Citrus Herb Swordfish
- Ocean Bounty Seafood Paella
- King's Garlic Butter Lobster Tails
- Fisherman's Classic Clam Chowder
- Seaside Lemon Herb Shrimp Skewers
- Neptune's Spiced Crab Cakes
- Golden Fried Calamari Rings
- Roasted Garlic and White Wine Mussels
- Deep-Sea Blackened Tuna Steaks
- Mariner's Bourbon Glazed Salmon
- Coastal Coconut Shrimp Curry
- Ocean Pearl Scallop Ceviche
- Fisherman's Beer-Battered Fish and Chips
- Sun-Dried Tomato and Anchovy Pasta
- Sea Breeze Grilled Octopus
- Sailor's Smoked Mackerel Spread
- Islander's Pineapple Glazed Mahi-Mahi
- Deep Blue Lobster Bisque
- Mediterranean Herb-Crusted Snapper
- Tidal Wave Spicy Seafood Gumbo
- Marinated Grilled Sardines with Lemon Zest
- Spicy Sriracha Honey Shrimp
- Castaway's Coconut Lime Halibut
- Rustic Fisherman's Stew
- Salt Crusted Whole Branzino
- White Wine Garlic Butter Clams
- Golden Brown Tuna Croquettes
- Seafarer's Seaweed-Wrapped Sushi Rolls
- Lemon Dill Buttered Crab Legs
- Oceanic Baked Cod with Herb Crust
- Lighthouse Lobster Mac and Cheese
- Citrus Seared Scallops with Mango Salsa
- Caribbean Jerk Grilled Snapper
- Fiery Cajun Blackened Catfish
- Island-Style Ginger Lime Prawns

- Fisherman's Harvest Tuna Niçoise Salad
- Dockside Grilled Oysters with Parmesan
- King's Smoked Salmon Bagel Spread
- Sunset Bay Shrimp and Avocado Ceviche
- Lighthouse Spicy Clam Linguine
- Thai Coconut Lemongrass Mussels
- Citrus Butter Poached Lobster
- Hearty Tomato Basil Bouillabaisse
- Captain's Spiced Fish Tacos
- Zesty Grilled Mahi-Mahi with Corn Salsa
- Honey Glazed Teriyaki Salmon Skewers
- Balsamic Roasted Sardines with Capers
- Seaside Dill and Lemon Smoked Trout
- Golden Fried Soft Shell Crab Sandwich
- New England Clam Bake Feast

Grilled Citrus Herb Swordfish

Ingredients:

- 2 swordfish steaks
- 2 tbsp olive oil
- 1 lemon, zested and juiced
- 1 orange, zested and juiced
- 2 cloves garlic, minced
- 1 tbsp fresh thyme, chopped
- 1 tsp sea salt
- ½ tsp black pepper

Instructions:

1. In a bowl, whisk olive oil, citrus zest, juices, garlic, thyme, salt, and pepper.
2. Marinate swordfish steaks for 30 minutes.
3. Preheat grill to medium-high heat.
4. Grill for 4-5 minutes per side until cooked through.
5. Serve with additional lemon wedges.

Ocean Bounty Seafood Paella

Ingredients:

- 1 ½ cups Arborio rice
- 3 cups seafood broth
- 1 lb mixed seafood (shrimp, mussels, clams, squid)
- 1 small onion, diced
- 2 cloves garlic, minced
- 1 tsp smoked paprika
- ½ tsp saffron threads
- 1 cup diced tomatoes
- ½ cup peas
- 2 tbsp olive oil
- ¼ cup chopped parsley

Instructions:

1. Heat olive oil in a large pan over medium heat. Sauté onion and garlic until soft.
2. Stir in rice, paprika, and saffron. Cook for 2 minutes.
3. Add tomatoes and broth. Simmer for 15 minutes.
4. Add seafood and peas. Cover and cook for 5-7 minutes.
5. Garnish with parsley and serve.

King's Garlic Butter Lobster Tails

Ingredients:

- 2 lobster tails
- 3 tbsp butter, melted
- 2 cloves garlic, minced
- 1 tbsp lemon juice
- ½ tsp paprika
- ¼ tsp salt
- ¼ tsp black pepper
- Fresh parsley for garnish

Instructions:

1. Preheat oven to 425°F (220°C).
2. Split lobster tails and gently lift the meat from the shell.
3. Mix butter, garlic, lemon juice, paprika, salt, and pepper.
4. Brush over the lobster meat and bake for 10-12 minutes.
5. Garnish with parsley and serve with extra butter.

Fisherman's Classic Clam Chowder

Ingredients:

- 2 cups chopped clams
- 3 cups clam juice
- 2 cups diced potatoes
- 1 small onion, chopped
- 2 cloves garlic, minced
- 2 tbsp butter
- 2 tbsp flour
- 1 cup heavy cream
- ½ tsp thyme
- ½ tsp salt
- ¼ tsp black pepper

Instructions:

1. In a pot, melt butter and sauté onion and garlic until soft.
2. Stir in flour and cook for 1 minute.
3. Gradually add clam juice, then potatoes. Simmer until potatoes are tender.
4. Add clams, cream, thyme, salt, and pepper. Simmer for 5 minutes.
5. Serve warm with crusty bread.

Seaside Lemon Herb Shrimp Skewers

Ingredients:

- 1 lb shrimp, peeled and deveined
- 2 tbsp olive oil
- 1 lemon, zested and juiced
- 2 cloves garlic, minced
- 1 tbsp fresh parsley, chopped
- ½ tsp salt
- ½ tsp black pepper

Instructions:

1. In a bowl, mix olive oil, lemon zest, juice, garlic, parsley, salt, and pepper.
2. Toss shrimp in marinade and let sit for 15 minutes.
3. Thread shrimp onto skewers and grill for 2-3 minutes per side.

Neptune's Spiced Crab Cakes

Ingredients:

- 1 lb lump crab meat
- ½ cup breadcrumbs
- 1 egg, beaten
- 2 tbsp mayonnaise
- 1 tsp Dijon mustard
- 1 tsp Old Bay seasoning
- 1 tbsp fresh parsley, chopped
- 1 tbsp butter (for frying)

Instructions:

1. In a bowl, mix all ingredients except butter.
2. Shape into small patties.
3. Heat butter in a pan and cook crab cakes for 3-4 minutes per side until golden brown.

Golden Fried Calamari Rings

Ingredients:

- 1 lb squid, sliced into rings
- ½ cup flour
- ½ cup cornstarch
- 1 tsp paprika
- ½ tsp salt
- ½ tsp black pepper
- Oil for frying
- Lemon wedges for serving

Instructions:

1. Heat oil to 375°F (190°C).
2. Mix flour, cornstarch, paprika, salt, and pepper in a bowl.
3. Dredge squid rings in the mixture.
4. Fry in batches for 2-3 minutes until golden. Drain on paper towels.
5. Serve with lemon wedges.

Roasted Garlic and White Wine Mussels

Ingredients:

- 2 lbs mussels, cleaned
- 2 tbsp olive oil
- 4 cloves garlic, minced
- 1 cup white wine
- 2 tbsp butter
- 1 tbsp fresh parsley, chopped
- ½ tsp red pepper flakes

Instructions:

1. Heat olive oil in a large pot. Sauté garlic for 1 minute.
2. Add white wine and bring to a simmer.
3. Add mussels, cover, and steam for 5 minutes until they open.
4. Stir in butter, parsley, and red pepper flakes. Serve warm.

Deep-Sea Blackened Tuna Steaks

Ingredients:

- 2 tuna steaks
- 1 tbsp olive oil
- 1 tsp smoked paprika
- 1 tsp garlic powder
- ½ tsp cayenne pepper
- ½ tsp salt
- ½ tsp black pepper

Instructions:

1. Mix spices together and rub over tuna steaks.
2. Heat oil in a pan over high heat.
3. Sear tuna for 1-2 minutes per side for medium-rare.
4. Serve with a fresh salad or rice.

Mariner's Bourbon Glazed Salmon

Ingredients:

- 2 salmon fillets
- ¼ cup bourbon
- 2 tbsp soy sauce
- 2 tbsp brown sugar
- 1 tbsp Dijon mustard
- 1 tbsp olive oil
- 1 clove garlic, minced

Instructions:

1. Mix bourbon, soy sauce, brown sugar, mustard, olive oil, and garlic.
2. Marinate salmon for 30 minutes.
3. Preheat grill to medium heat and cook salmon for 4-5 minutes per side.

Coastal Coconut Shrimp Curry

Ingredients:

- 1 lb shrimp, peeled and deveined
- 1 can (14 oz) coconut milk
- 1 small onion, chopped
- 2 cloves garlic, minced
- 1 tbsp ginger, grated
- 1 tbsp red curry paste
- 1 tsp turmeric
- 1 tsp cumin
- 1 tbsp fish sauce
- 1 tbsp lime juice
- 1 tbsp oil
- ½ cup chopped cilantro

Instructions:

1. Heat oil in a pan over medium heat. Sauté onion, garlic, and ginger.
2. Stir in curry paste, turmeric, and cumin. Cook for 1 minute.
3. Pour in coconut milk and bring to a simmer.
4. Add shrimp and cook for 3-4 minutes.
5. Stir in fish sauce and lime juice. Garnish with cilantro.

Ocean Pearl Scallop Ceviche

Ingredients:

- ½ lb fresh scallops, diced
- ½ cup lime juice
- 1 small red onion, finely chopped
- 1 jalapeño, minced
- ½ cup diced mango
- ¼ cup chopped cilantro
- ½ tsp salt

Instructions:

1. In a bowl, mix scallops with lime juice and refrigerate for 30 minutes.
2. Stir in onion, jalapeño, mango, cilantro, and salt.
3. Chill for another 10 minutes before serving.

Fisherman's Beer-Battered Fish and Chips

Ingredients:

- 1 lb white fish (cod, haddock), cut into fillets
- 1 cup flour
- 1 cup beer (lager or ale)
- 1 tsp baking powder
- ½ tsp salt
- ½ tsp paprika
- Oil for frying
- 2 large potatoes, cut into fries

Instructions:

1. Heat oil to 375°F (190°C).
2. Mix flour, beer, baking powder, salt, and paprika.
3. Dip fish in batter and fry for 4-5 minutes until golden.
4. Fry potatoes until crispy. Serve with tartar sauce.

Sun-Dried Tomato and Anchovy Pasta

Ingredients:

- 8 oz spaghetti
- 2 tbsp olive oil
- 3 cloves garlic, minced
- 4 anchovy fillets, chopped
- ½ cup sun-dried tomatoes, sliced
- ½ tsp red pepper flakes
- ¼ cup grated Parmesan
- 2 tbsp chopped parsley

Instructions:

1. Cook spaghetti according to package instructions.
2. Heat olive oil and sauté garlic, anchovies, and red pepper flakes.
3. Stir in sun-dried tomatoes and cooked pasta.
4. Toss with Parmesan and parsley.

Sea Breeze Grilled Octopus

Ingredients:

- 1 lb octopus, cleaned
- ¼ cup olive oil
- 2 tbsp lemon juice
- 2 cloves garlic, minced
- 1 tsp smoked paprika
- ½ tsp salt
- ½ tsp black pepper

Instructions:

1. Boil octopus in salted water for 45 minutes until tender.
2. Marinate in olive oil, lemon juice, garlic, paprika, salt, and pepper.
3. Grill for 2-3 minutes per side.

Sailor's Smoked Mackerel Spread

Ingredients:

- 1 cup smoked mackerel, flaked
- ½ cup cream cheese
- 2 tbsp sour cream
- 1 tbsp lemon juice
- 1 tbsp fresh dill, chopped
- ½ tsp black pepper

Instructions:

1. Blend all ingredients until smooth.
2. Chill before serving with crackers or toast.

Islander's Pineapple Glazed Mahi-Mahi

Ingredients:

- 2 mahi-mahi fillets
- ½ cup pineapple juice
- 2 tbsp honey
- 1 tbsp soy sauce
- 1 clove garlic, minced
- ½ tsp ginger, grated

Instructions:

1. Mix pineapple juice, honey, soy sauce, garlic, and ginger.
2. Marinate mahi-mahi for 30 minutes.
3. Grill over medium heat for 4-5 minutes per side.

Deep Blue Lobster Bisque

Ingredients:

- 2 lobster tails, cooked and chopped
- 2 tbsp butter
- 1 small onion, diced
- 1 clove garlic, minced
- 2 tbsp tomato paste
- 1 cup seafood stock
- ½ cup heavy cream
- ¼ tsp cayenne pepper
- ½ tsp salt

Instructions:

1. Sauté onion and garlic in butter. Stir in tomato paste.
2. Add seafood stock and simmer for 10 minutes.
3. Blend until smooth, return to heat, and stir in cream.
4. Add lobster and simmer for 5 minutes.

Mediterranean Herb-Crusted Snapper

Ingredients:

- 2 snapper fillets
- 2 tbsp olive oil
- ¼ cup breadcrumbs
- 1 tbsp fresh parsley, chopped
- 1 tbsp fresh basil, chopped
- 1 tsp lemon zest
- ½ tsp salt
- ½ tsp black pepper

Instructions:

1. Mix breadcrumbs, parsley, basil, lemon zest, salt, and pepper.
2. Brush snapper with olive oil and coat with herb mixture.
3. Bake at 375°F (190°C) for 12-15 minutes.

Tidal Wave Spicy Seafood Gumbo

Ingredients:

- ½ lb shrimp, peeled and deveined
- ½ lb crab meat
- ½ lb andouille sausage, sliced
- ½ cup flour
- ½ cup butter
- 1 onion, chopped
- 1 bell pepper, chopped
- 2 celery stalks, chopped
- 3 cloves garlic, minced
- 4 cups seafood stock
- 1 can (14 oz) diced tomatoes
- 1 tbsp Cajun seasoning
- 1 tsp cayenne pepper
- 1 bay leaf
- 2 tbsp chopped parsley

Instructions:

1. Make a roux by whisking butter and flour over medium heat until golden brown.
2. Add onion, bell pepper, celery, and garlic. Sauté until soft.
3. Stir in sausage, seafood stock, tomatoes, and seasonings. Simmer for 30 minutes.
4. Add shrimp and crab, cooking for another 5 minutes.
5. Serve hot with rice, garnished with parsley.

Marinated Grilled Sardines with Lemon Zest

Ingredients:

- 6 fresh sardines, cleaned
- ¼ cup olive oil
- 2 tbsp lemon juice
- 1 tsp lemon zest
- 2 cloves garlic, minced
- ½ tsp smoked paprika
- ½ tsp salt

Instructions:

1. Mix olive oil, lemon juice, zest, garlic, paprika, and salt.
2. Marinate sardines for 30 minutes.
3. Grill over medium heat for 3-4 minutes per side.

Spicy Sriracha Honey Shrimp

Ingredients:

- 1 lb shrimp, peeled and deveined
- ¼ cup honey
- 2 tbsp Sriracha sauce
- 2 tbsp soy sauce
- 1 tbsp lime juice
- 1 clove garlic, minced

Instructions:

1. Whisk honey, Sriracha, soy sauce, lime juice, and garlic.
2. Marinate shrimp for 15 minutes.
3. Sauté or grill for 2-3 minutes per side.

Castaway's Coconut Lime Halibut

Ingredients:

- 2 halibut fillets
- ½ cup coconut milk
- 1 tbsp lime juice
- 1 tsp lime zest
- ½ tsp salt
- ½ tsp black pepper

Instructions:

1. Marinate halibut in coconut milk, lime juice, zest, salt, and pepper for 20 minutes.
2. Sear over medium heat for 3-4 minutes per side.

Rustic Fisherman's Stew

Ingredients:

- ½ lb cod, cut into chunks
- ½ lb shrimp
- ½ cup white wine
- 4 cups seafood stock
- 1 onion, chopped
- 2 cloves garlic, minced
- 1 can (14 oz) diced tomatoes
- 1 tsp smoked paprika
- ½ tsp red pepper flakes
- 1 tbsp olive oil

Instructions:

1. Heat olive oil and sauté onion and garlic.
2. Add wine, stock, tomatoes, paprika, and red pepper flakes. Simmer for 15 minutes.
3. Stir in cod and shrimp, cooking for another 5 minutes.

Salt Crusted Whole Branzino

Ingredients:

- 1 whole branzino, cleaned
- 4 cups coarse sea salt
- 2 egg whites
- 1 lemon, sliced
- 2 sprigs fresh thyme

Instructions:

1. Stuff branzino with lemon and thyme.
2. Mix salt and egg whites, forming a thick paste.
3. Coat the fish entirely and bake at 400°F (200°C) for 25 minutes.
4. Crack the salt crust before serving.

White Wine Garlic Butter Clams

Ingredients:

- 1 lb fresh clams
- ½ cup white wine
- 2 tbsp butter
- 3 cloves garlic, minced
- 1 tbsp chopped parsley

Instructions:

1. Heat butter in a pan and sauté garlic.
2. Add clams and white wine. Cover and cook until clams open.
3. Garnish with parsley and serve.

Golden Brown Tuna Croquettes

Ingredients:

- 1 can (6 oz) tuna, drained
- ½ cup breadcrumbs
- 1 egg
- 2 tbsp mayonnaise
- 1 tsp Dijon mustard
- ½ tsp salt
- ½ tsp black pepper
- Oil for frying

Instructions:

1. Mix tuna, breadcrumbs, egg, mayonnaise, mustard, salt, and pepper.
2. Form into patties and chill for 15 minutes.
3. Pan-fry until golden brown.

Seafarer's Seaweed-Wrapped Sushi Rolls

Ingredients:

- 1 cup sushi rice, cooked
- 2 tbsp rice vinegar
- 4 nori seaweed sheets
- ½ cucumber, julienned
- ½ avocado, sliced
- 4 oz fresh tuna or salmon, sliced

Instructions:

1. Mix rice with vinegar.
2. Spread rice on nori sheets, leaving a 1-inch border.
3. Add cucumber, avocado, and fish.
4. Roll tightly and slice.

Lemon Dill Buttered Crab Legs

Ingredients:

- 1 lb crab legs
- ¼ cup butter, melted
- 1 tbsp lemon juice
- 1 tsp fresh dill, chopped

Instructions:

1. Steam crab legs for 5 minutes.
2. Mix butter, lemon juice, and dill.
3. Serve with crab legs.

Oceanic Baked Cod with Herb Crust

Ingredients:

- 2 cod fillets
- ½ cup breadcrumbs
- 2 tbsp fresh parsley, chopped
- 1 tbsp fresh thyme, chopped
- 2 cloves garlic, minced
- 2 tbsp olive oil
- 1 tbsp lemon juice
- ½ tsp salt
- ½ tsp black pepper

Instructions:

1. Preheat oven to 375°F (190°C).
2. Mix breadcrumbs, parsley, thyme, garlic, olive oil, lemon juice, salt, and pepper.
3. Coat the cod with the herb mixture and bake for 15 minutes.

Lighthouse Lobster Mac and Cheese

Ingredients:

- 8 oz elbow macaroni
- 1 cup cooked lobster meat, chopped
- 2 cups shredded cheddar cheese
- 1 cup shredded Gruyère cheese
- 2 cups milk
- 2 tbsp butter
- 2 tbsp flour
- ½ tsp paprika
- ½ cup panko breadcrumbs

Instructions:

1. Cook macaroni according to package instructions.
2. Melt butter, whisk in flour, and cook for 1 minute.
3. Slowly add milk, then stir in cheese and paprika.
4. Mix in macaroni and lobster, then top with panko.
5. Bake at 375°F (190°C) for 20 minutes.

Citrus Seared Scallops with Mango Salsa

Ingredients:

- 8 large scallops
- 1 tbsp olive oil
- 1 tbsp orange zest
- ½ tsp salt
- ½ tsp black pepper
- ½ cup diced mango
- ¼ cup diced red onion
- 1 tbsp lime juice
- 1 tbsp chopped cilantro

Instructions:

1. Mix mango, onion, lime juice, and cilantro for salsa.
2. Season scallops with salt, pepper, and orange zest.
3. Sear scallops in olive oil for 2 minutes per side.
4. Serve with mango salsa.

Caribbean Jerk Grilled Snapper

Ingredients:

- 2 snapper fillets
- 1 tbsp jerk seasoning
- 1 tbsp olive oil
- 1 tbsp lime juice

Instructions:

1. Rub snapper with jerk seasoning, oil, and lime juice.
2. Grill over medium heat for 4 minutes per side.

Fiery Cajun Blackened Catfish

Ingredients:

- 2 catfish fillets
- 1 tbsp Cajun seasoning
- 1 tbsp olive oil
- ½ tsp smoked paprika

Instructions:

1. Coat catfish with Cajun seasoning and paprika.
2. Sear in hot oil for 3 minutes per side.

Island-Style Ginger Lime Prawns

Ingredients:

- 1 lb prawns, peeled
- 2 tbsp soy sauce
- 1 tbsp grated ginger
- 1 tbsp lime juice
- 1 tbsp honey

Instructions:

1. Marinate prawns in soy sauce, ginger, lime juice, and honey for 15 minutes.
2. Sauté or grill for 2 minutes per side.

Fisherman's Harvest Tuna Niçoise Salad

Ingredients:

- 1 tuna steak
- 1 cup baby potatoes, boiled
- ½ cup green beans, blanched
- ½ cup cherry tomatoes, halved
- 1 boiled egg, sliced
- ¼ cup olives
- 2 tbsp olive oil
- 1 tbsp Dijon mustard
- 1 tbsp lemon juice

Instructions:

1. Sear tuna for 2 minutes per side.
2. Mix salad ingredients and top with sliced tuna.
3. Whisk olive oil, mustard, and lemon juice for dressing.

Dockside Grilled Oysters with Parmesan

Ingredients:

- 6 fresh oysters
- ¼ cup grated Parmesan
- 2 tbsp butter, melted
- 1 tbsp chopped parsley

Instructions:

1. Top oysters with butter and Parmesan.
2. Grill for 3 minutes until bubbly.

King's Smoked Salmon Bagel Spread

Ingredients:

- 4 oz smoked salmon, chopped
- 8 oz cream cheese
- 1 tbsp capers
- 1 tbsp lemon juice
- 1 tbsp chopped dill

Instructions:

1. Mix all ingredients until smooth.
2. Serve on bagels.

Sunset Bay Shrimp and Avocado Ceviche

Ingredients:

- ½ lb shrimp, diced
- ½ cup lime juice
- ½ avocado, diced
- ½ cup diced tomatoes
- ¼ cup red onion, diced
- 1 tbsp cilantro

Instructions:

1. Marinate shrimp in lime juice for 30 minutes.
2. Mix with other ingredients and serve.

Lighthouse Spicy Clam Linguine

Ingredients:

- 8 oz linguine
- 1 lb fresh clams, cleaned
- 3 cloves garlic, minced
- 1 tsp red pepper flakes
- ½ cup white wine
- 2 tbsp olive oil
- 2 tbsp fresh parsley, chopped
- Juice of 1 lemon

Instructions:

1. Cook linguine according to package instructions.
2. Sauté garlic and red pepper flakes in olive oil.
3. Add clams and white wine, cover, and cook until clams open (5-7 minutes).
4. Toss with linguine, lemon juice, and parsley.

Thai Coconut Lemongrass Mussels

Ingredients:

- 1 lb mussels, cleaned
- 1 can (13.5 oz) coconut milk
- 1 stalk lemongrass, minced
- 2 cloves garlic, minced
- 1 tbsp ginger, grated
- 1 tbsp fish sauce
- 1 lime, juiced
- 1 tbsp cilantro, chopped

Instructions:

1. Sauté lemongrass, garlic, and ginger in a pot.
2. Add coconut milk and fish sauce, bring to a simmer.
3. Add mussels and cook covered until they open (5 minutes).
4. Stir in lime juice and cilantro before serving.

Citrus Butter Poached Lobster

Ingredients:

- 2 lobster tails
- ½ cup butter
- Zest and juice of 1 orange
- 1 tsp lemon zest
- ½ tsp salt

Instructions:

1. Melt butter with citrus zest and juice over low heat.
2. Add lobster tails and poach for 6-8 minutes.

Hearty Tomato Basil Bouillabaisse

Ingredients:

- ½ lb white fish, cubed
- ½ lb shrimp, peeled
- 1 lb clams
- 3 cups fish stock
- 1 can (14 oz) diced tomatoes
- ½ cup white wine
- 1 onion, chopped
- 2 cloves garlic, minced
- 1 tbsp fresh basil

Instructions:

1. Sauté onion and garlic in olive oil.
2. Add wine, stock, and tomatoes; simmer for 10 minutes.
3. Add seafood and cook until done (5 minutes).
4. Garnish with basil.

Captain's Spiced Fish Tacos

Ingredients:

- 2 fish fillets (cod or mahi-mahi)
- 1 tbsp taco seasoning
- 1 tbsp olive oil
- 4 small tortillas
- ½ cup shredded cabbage
- ¼ cup sour cream
- Juice of 1 lime

Instructions:

1. Season fish and cook in olive oil for 4 minutes per side.
2. Assemble tacos with cabbage, fish, sour cream, and lime juice.

Zesty Grilled Mahi-Mahi with Corn Salsa

Ingredients:

- 2 mahi-mahi fillets
- 1 tbsp olive oil
- 1 tsp chili powder
- ½ cup corn
- ¼ cup diced red bell pepper
- 1 tbsp lime juice

Instructions:

1. Grill mahi-mahi with olive oil and chili powder for 5 minutes per side.
2. Mix corn, bell pepper, and lime juice for salsa.

Honey Glazed Teriyaki Salmon Skewers

Ingredients:

- 1 lb salmon, cubed
- ¼ cup teriyaki sauce
- 1 tbsp honey
- 1 tsp sesame seeds

Instructions:

1. Marinate salmon in teriyaki and honey for 30 minutes.
2. Skewer and grill for 4 minutes per side.
3. Sprinkle with sesame seeds before serving.

Balsamic Roasted Sardines with Capers

Ingredients:

- 4 whole sardines, cleaned
- 1 tbsp olive oil
- 1 tbsp balsamic vinegar
- 1 tbsp capers

Instructions:

1. Toss sardines with oil, balsamic, and capers.
2. Roast at 400°F (200°C) for 10 minutes.

Seaside Dill and Lemon Smoked Trout

Ingredients:

- 1 smoked trout fillet
- 1 tbsp fresh dill, chopped
- Juice of 1 lemon

Instructions:

1. Flake trout and toss with dill and lemon juice.
2. Serve chilled or as a spread.

Golden Fried Soft Shell Crab Sandwich

Ingredients:

- 2 soft shell crabs
- ½ cup flour
- ½ tsp Old Bay seasoning
- 1 egg, beaten
- ½ cup breadcrumbs
- 2 sandwich buns
- ¼ cup tartar sauce

Instructions:

1. Coat crabs in flour, egg, then breadcrumbs.
2. Fry for 3 minutes per side.
3. Serve on buns with tartar sauce.

New England Clam Bake Feast

Ingredients:

- 1 lb clams
- 1 lb mussels
- 1 lb shrimp
- 2 ears corn, cut into thirds
- 2 small potatoes, halved
- 2 tbsp Old Bay seasoning
- ½ cup white wine

Instructions:

1. Steam all ingredients with white wine and Old Bay for 10 minutes.

www.ingramcontent.com/pod-product-compliance
Lightning Source LLC
LaVergne TN
LVHW081340060526
838201LV00055B/2772